A true lady is always faultlessly neat.

No richness of dress in the afternoon, no diamonds in the evening, can atone for unbrushed hair, a soiled collar, or untidy slippers at breakfast!

The Etiquette of Dress

Compiled by
Madeleine Brant

Copper Beech Publishing

Published in Great Britain by
Copper Beech Publishing Ltd

ISBN 1 898617 11 2

A CIP catalogue record for this book is available from the British Library.

Editor: Jan Barnes
Special thanks to Hazel Mitchell and Beryl Peters for use of material from their private collections.
Some line illustrations used courtesy of Port Sunlight Heritage Centre, Wirral.

Copper Beech Gift Books
Copper Beech Publishing Ltd
P O Box 159 East Grinstead
Sussex England RH19 4FS

Good clothes open all doors.
Thomas Fuller 1705

INTRODUCTION

'A lady can be badly dressed with a fortune, or well-dressed on a modest income.'

Men may laugh at a woman facing the problem of what she should wear. However, all women understand the anxiety caused when attempting to choose the right outfit for any occasion.

Writers have advised women on how to be well dressed for over 150 years. Fashions come and go, but the essential rules of good dressing remain the same.

Above all, dress should be appropriate to the occasion and to the wearer, regardless of rank and wealth. Dress should enhance her figure and flatter her colouring, while concealing any 'little imperfections'.

This is as true for the duchess as for her dairymaid.

To be well dressed is not a matter of showy finery, least of all fake jewels and imitation lace, but of well chosen and well fitting clothes, kept neat and in good repair.

The hints contained herein have been compiled from the works of late Victorian and Edwardian writers, but their message is still relevant to everyone who would be thought well dressed, regardless of time or fashion.

The advice which follows will both entertain and inform, and should prove invaluable to any woman who wishes to impress her friends, but not frighten her horses!

Madeleine Brant

There are certain occasions
when it is your duty to dress – when
an indifferent toilette is a rudeness to those
you are in company with.

DRESS FOR OCCASIONS

If you are invited to stay on a visit, you must be nicely dressed from morning till night!

The etiquette of dress is easy to acquire.

If you are invited to a friend's wedding you should put on a nice dress to do her honour.

If a friend offers to take you to a theatre, it is equally necessary that you should be well appointed.

A good appearance is as essential a part of respect to your host as a proper consideration for yourself.

Whilst speaking on the subject of suitability in dress, it may be well to mention that Sunday can make an exception to any rule.

If you are staying in a friend's house on Sunday, it is proper to come down to breakfast in the same dress you intend to wear at church, and it would be absurd to put on another for so short a time!

THE MORNING

Let the style of your dress be appropriate to the hour of the day.

To dress too finely in the morning, - or to be seen in a morning dress in the evening, is equally vulgar and out of place.

Light and inexpensive materials are fittest for morning wear; a lady cannot dress with too much simplicity in the early part of the day.

A morning dress of some simple material, and delicate whole colour, with collar and cuffs of spotless linen, is, perhaps, the most becoming and elegant of morning toilettes.

The peril of being induced to wear ornaments in the morning is to be avoided, particularly to be dreaded in that class of society below the peeress's rank.

Every ornament on the head
is in bad taste in the morning;
one views with horror
huge gold pins, or would-be gold,
corresponding to earrings of the
same false description!

WALKING DRESS

With the correct costume a lady may enjoy the pleasures of a walk in a muddy lane.

In a town, according to the time of the day, or time of the year, a walking dress should be simple, yet there should still be some degree of richness in the dress.

In the country, the attire should be tasteful, solid and strong. The bonnet may still be becoming though plain, perhaps of straw or whalebone.

Cloaks of a light material for summer, and stout in the winter, are more elegant and suitable than shawls which belong rather to the carriage or visiting dress.

With warm cloak, looped dress, shady hat and soft gloves to complete a country walking costume, the high-born lady may enjoy the privileges which her inferiors already possess - she may take a good walk with pleasure and safety, and not shudder at the aspect of a muddy lane!

RIDING DRESS

Too long a skirt is apt to alarm the horses!

Compactness and utility are the requisites for the riding dress; and, whilst touching on this point, let us impress strongly the danger arising from too long a skirt in the riding-habit.

Too long a skirt is apt not only to alarm the horses, but to entangle, in case of accidents, their fair riders!

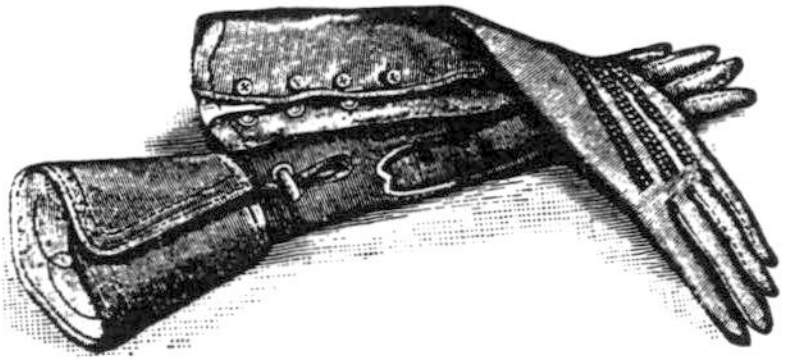

As far as a riding costume is concerned, nothing secures the freshness of the face better than the slouched hat. It is cool, and permits the free circulation of air around the face, while it protects the eyes, the forehead, and almost the chin, from scorching heat or withering blasts!

THE CARRIAGE OR VISITING DRESS

The carriage or visiting dress should be exceedingly handsome.

The visiting dress should be gayer in colour, richer in texture than the morning dress at home.

In summer all should be light, cool, agreeable to think of, pleasant to look at.

Nothing can be in worse taste than to keep on the warm clothing of winter, after winter and even spring have gone.

Light scarves in muslin are especially elegant. Delicate silks are infinitely more suitable to summer and its bright hours, than the heavy cashmeres and velvets, be they ever so handsome.

DRESS FOR AFTERNOON PARTIES

Occasions when a woman may feel some hesitation.

Although the rules about the etiquette of dress are so simple, there are occasions on which a woman may be excused for feeling some hesitation.

Hostesses, anxious to provide some novel entertainment, send out invitations which can often plunge their recipients into a state of embarrassment.

No-one who has ever been either over-dressed or under-dressed at an afternoon party is ever likely to forget it!

To be suitably dressed is worth bestowing some thought upon, particularly if you receive an invitation, the hours being between three til seven.

In all such cases the rule is clear - as long as the hours specified are before seven, it is plain that *evening dress cannot be required.*

IN THE COUNTRY

The same dress is worn until five o'clock tea!

Day dress in the country is generally considerably plainer. There is not the same necessity for a change of attire in the afternoon as there is in town.

There is no occasion to discard the morning toilette at luncheon. The same dress is generally worn until five o'clock tea, when a tea-gown is generally adopted during the few hours that are spent in the boudoir before dressing for dinner.

Well-bred persons do not make an elaborate toilette in the daytime in the country unless there is some reason for it!

EVENING COSTUME AT HOME

There is something in exposing the bare shoulders and arms to the glare of day, that startles an observer!

People in society are supposed to dress for dinner, and wherever they go afterwards they are naturally in evening dress.

The dinner hour governs society as far as the etiquette of dress is concerned.

The ordinary evening costume at home admits of great taste and becomingness. In some great houses it differs little from that assumed at large dinner parties, except that ornaments are less worn.

A low dress is by far the most becoming, according to age, complexion, and the style of the house - a point always to be taken into consideration. Yet a lady should restrict this to dinners by candle light.

In summer a thin high dress, at any rate, is more convenient and more modest.

For all occasions a lady of rank and fortune should have her separate dresses.

She should not wear out her old ball or dinner dresses by her fireside at home and in intimate circles. They always have a tawdry, miserable look.

Nothing is so vulgar as finery out of place!

The full dinner-dress demands great splendour. The dress may be blue, silver-grey, maize, lavender, or (but rare) very pale green; pink is suitable alone to balls.

The dinner dresses that last for ever are detestable!

BALL DRESSES

The lighter and more ethereal-looking the fabric, the more successful a ball dress will be.

The great point to be aimed at in a ball dress is to get something that will look striking on entering the room and yet look neat when leaving it.

Ball gowns should always be of light delicate colours, the soft flimsy materials such as chiffon, ninon and net being the prettiest and the most graceful for these occasions.

The gloves worn with these gowns are extremely long, covering the whole of the arm; and shoes and stockings worn to match.

DRESS FOR THE WOMAN WORKER

A business woman, engaged from morning to night, is hindered by lack of the time in which to select and care for her clothes.

The women workers in our large cities are apt to err most lamentably in regard to their dress in office hours.

Girl typists will be seen dressed in light fluffy dresses, with short sleeves and no collars, their dress liberally adorned with imitation jewellery.

Such a dress is thoroughly out of place in a business office. The girl who adopts it will do herself a great disservice when it comes to the question of seeking for a new post!

Should the woman worker's office happen to be situated near the shopping quarter she may certainly be able to give up her lunch hour to the purchase of materials, or of a coat or costume.

Unless the 'hour' is an elastic term it does not allow much time for comparison or choice.

At the end of her day's work, the best shops are closed, or on the point of closing, and it means, in winter at least, buying by artificial light.

An occasional walk round to look at the goods displayed in the windows, either at lunch-time, or in the evening, or Saturday afternoon, when many windows are obligingly left unshuttered, is by no means a waste of time, as it gives an idea of what is being stocked, and where the best value can be obtained.

Appearances go for a great deal in business, as much in fact as under any other conditions of life!

TASTE

There is no doubt that dress is a very fair index of the mind of the wearer.

In dress, as in most other things, there are two kinds of taste: good taste and bad taste. We use the word 'taste' in a sense quite distinct from 'style'.

It is a disputed point whether really good taste can ever be acquired, or whether it is only inherent.

What offends against good taste is much easier to point out than to say in so many words in what good taste consists.

Fashion prescribes rules for all. The fine lady who frequents the court - as well as the servant girl who sweeps out a London lodging-house, and all the intermediate classes, can be guided by fashion rather than taste.

Fashion can suggest the size and shape of hats, the make of gowns, their length and their size, the trimmings, the petticoats and all the other paraphernalia of a lady's toilette.

STYLE

Suitability is half the secret of dress and the most perfect toilette donned under the wrong conditions only succeeds in being a perfect failure!

Every woman is possessed of a certain distinctiveness of appearance which, for the want of a better word, we call her 'style'.

One woman looks best in long luxurious robes, whilst another never looks so well as in a tailor-made gown with a linen collar. One woman shows to advantage in a tea-gown whilst another who has what is called an 'interesting' appearance, seems naturally to suit a black dress and a bunch of violets.

A woman is perfectly right in considering her style and in carefully moulding her dress to correspond. But whilst society allows every latitude concerning what you shall wear, it is extremely rigorous about *when* you shall wear it!

It is in the accessories of her dress that the well dressed woman justifies her reputation as such.

GLOVES BOOTS AND SHOES

One can always tell a lady by her gloves and her shoes.

Gloves should 'fit like a glove', be of good colour, according well with the rest of the costume, neither too light nor too dark, but rather light than dark.

There should be no ends or corners of the fingers which are not well filled; nor any creases indicative of the gloves being of a wrong size, or put on crooked, with a twist given to the fingers, so that the seams of the glove do not appear straight.

Over a plump hand gloves should fit comfortably.

A woman with large hands should avoid light, shiny gloves. If she must wear light coloured gloves, those of suede look smaller than shiny kid ones

To be 'down at heel' is perhaps the worst form of shabbiness and the woman who goes about with holes in her gloves advertises the fact that she is lacking in that refinement.

Cheap boots are usually made of hard unyielding material; they are not only answerable for corns, bunions, blisters, and other similar ills, but their soles are little more effective than brown paper in resisting damp and wet - consequently many a severe chill and illness can be traced to their wear!

It is better to pay a good price for all boots and shoes, and the result will be much more satisfactory in the long-run.

There should not be much difficulty in getting ready-made boots to fit nowadays, when half and even quarter sizes are to be had.

There are many false economies habitually practised by various households; but of all false economies, economy in footwear is apt to become the dearest in the long-run.

With regard to shoes, there are several important points to mention. Low-heeled shoes never look well with a smart gown: there is nothing injurious about moderately high heels for house-wear, and they give a smart touch which few women can afford to dispense with.

Several good makes of walking shoes can be had for a modest sum. The cult of the 'small' foot is not as universal as it was a few years ago.

Women seldom nowadays are seen to attempt to squeeze their feet into shoes one or two sizes too small for them!

A woman with a naturally large foot would, however, do well always to wear her boots with toe-caps, as these diminish the apparent size of the foot; she should never wear brown and other light-coloured boots or shoes, as they have exactly the opposite effect.

Boots with very high heels and pointed toes should be avoided.

Evening shoes are worn to match the dress. They are usually of leather, suede or satin. Satin shoes are the most fashionable at the present moment.

Gold and silver leather evening shoes are also very smart, and can be worn with almost any evening gown.

Shoes or straps should never be tight if the feet are at all fat!

HATS AND BONNETS

The hat is truly the apex of the costume.

Small-featured women must never don picture hats; for them is the toque, and the neat-brimmed chapeau of all styles and ages.

Those with a regular outline of face may wear hats of the Gainsborough type, whilst those whose features, charming though they may be, are irregular, must adopt the 'floppy', 'any shape' style; though, provided the colouring be good enough, the hat may be as large as desired.

Those with retroussé noses should never wear hats with straight turned-down brims.

Big brims throw a shadow over the face, and, therefore, only those with brilliant colouring can withstand this effect.

Short women should adopt tall hats and lofty trimmings; low hats and flat trimming are not becoming.

People with large heads must wear good-sized bonnets, as nothing is more absurd than a bonnet perched like some strange ornament on a head of noble proportions!

JEWELLERY

Let your jewellery be always the best of its kind.

Love of jewellery is innate with almost all womankind.

Often at fashionable restaurants, a woman will be seen with diamond rings half covering every finger of both hands, sometimes not even excluding the thumbs!

Such a display may certainly be indicative of her wealth, but it serves even more to emphasise her lack of refinement and good breeding!

A great display of jewellery in the daytime is never in good taste.

For evening wear, however, one's taste for jewellery may be indulged, although excess should always be avoided.

There seems to be an inclination nowadays for women who cannot afford good jewellery to go in for various imitations and shams.

This is a *very* great mistake!

Sham jewellery is yet another unfailing sign of vulgarity! If a woman cannot afford diamonds and precious stones, she should be content with plain gold.

Too many rings are vulgar!

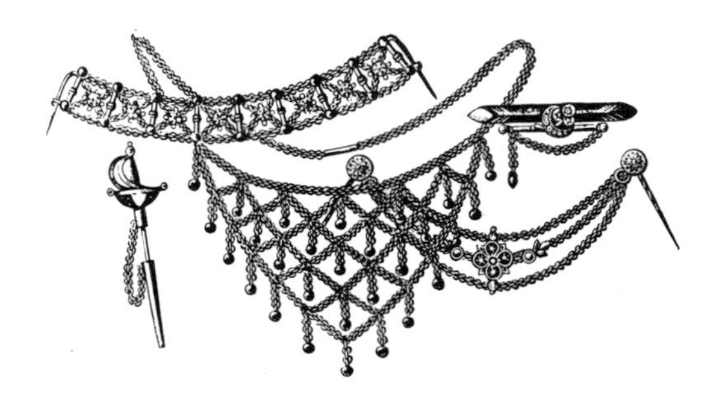

Just a little too much locket and bangle marks all the difference between a lady and a barmaid!

Dress is a very important matter to ladies. An untidily dressed person gives a constant feeling of discomfort to the beholder.

DRESSMAKERS' LORE

**A woman's neck should measure
twice the circumference of her wrist.
A woman's waist should measure
twice the circumference of her neck.**

UNDERGARMENTS

CORSETS
AND THE PERILS OF TIGHT LACING

If you lace tightly, nothing can save you from acquiring high shoulders, abnormally large hips, varicose veins in your legs, and a red nose!

No adult woman's waist ought to measure less in circumference than twenty-four inches at the smallest, and even this is permissible to slender figures only.

Corsets should support without constriction; they should be pliable and elastic. No man worth a woman's regard admires an unnatural waist.

Corsets should be made of perfectly permeable white canvas, stiff enough to afford comfortable support, while permitting free cutaneous evaporation; *wholly innocent of whalebones*, and having merely a very light steel busk, fastening easily in front.

These corsets should be made by a skilled artiste, and moulded to the figure.

Exquisite Models. Perfect Fit.
Guaranteed Wear.

THE Y & N

PATENT DIAGONAL

SEAM CORSETS

Will not split in the Seams nor tear in the Fabric.

"The most comfortable corsets ever made."—*Lady's Pictorial.*

Made in White, Black, and all the Fashionable Colours and Shades, in Italian Cloth, Satin, and Coutil.

4/11, 5/11, 6/11, 7/11

PER PAIR AND UPWARDS.

Sold by all principal Drapers and Ladies' Outfitters in United Kingdom and Colonies.

THREE GOLD MEDALS.

Lovely

FIGURE.

Should girls propose?—now the talk;—no need, Men fall on their knees to wearers of the CONFIGURATEUR CORSET, patent; transforms any **thin bust** to exquisitely lovely proportions of captivating (*natural*) beauty, impossible by any other Corset in the World. No hideous pads; stiffened breast (*hollow, hygienic*) regulates any desired fulness (intensely beautifies moderate figures). **French-Grey, 6/6; Black, 6/9; White or Black, 10/9**; 14ins. deep. Sent on approval, to test its *guaranteed* effect (plain parcel), post free, by **Patentees, BALE & Co.** (Dept. 10) **52, Aldermanbury, London, E.C.**

Send at once for circular; seldom advertised.

SHEWS BREAST

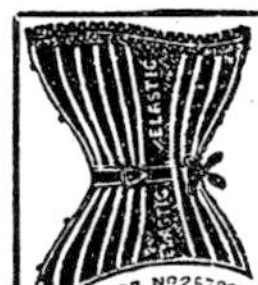

COMFORT CORSET.

OUR NEWEST INVENTION.

SMALL WAIST FOR ALL WITHOUT COMPRESSION.

Any Shape and Size. In Coutil, Sateen or Silk. *Write to-day for Illustrated List, Free.* Improved Cotton and Woollen Underclothing for all Climates for Ladies, Gentlemen and Children. Surgical Hosiery, Belts, etc. Mention *Home Notes.*

KNITTED CORSET & CLOTHING CO., 118, Mansfield Rd., Nottingham.

The petticoats should *not* be tied over the corset round the waist, thereby producing a bulky and ungainly effect, but attached to the edge of the corset low down on the hips, where the additional thickness is not disadvantageous.

Over the corset should be worn only a single under-bodice of spun silk. This occupies very little room, is warm, and so elastic that it may be fitted exactly over the stays, without wrinkling the dress.

It is always to be remembered, no girl should wear bones or steels until she has done growing.

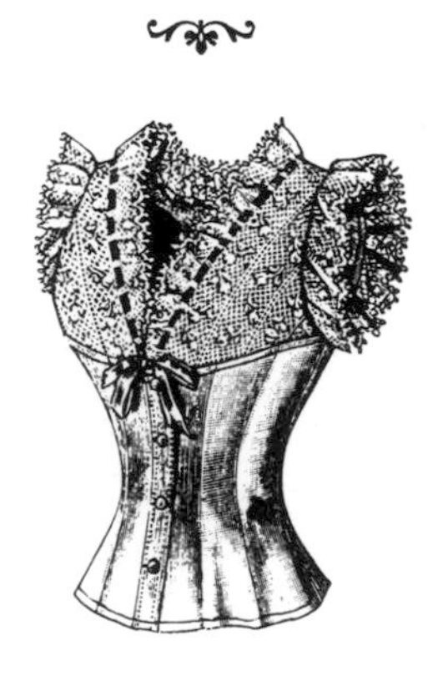

STOCKINGS

The finer the texture of the stockings the smarter are they supposed to be.

Cashmere stockings make the most satisfactory all-the-year round wear. Warm, closely woven cashmere stockings are suitable for the winter, and much lighter texture for the summer.

Those who wear lisle thread hose would always do well to see that the soles and heels are of cashmere. Stockings of this description can be had in a great many makes and from the point of view of both wear and comfort are far superior to those which are of lisle thread throughout.

When very fine lisle thread hose are woven quite plain without any pattern, the effect is that of fine silk.

Silk hosiery is undoubtedly the acme of 'dressiness' for very smart occasions.

SUSPENDERS

As a means of keeping up the stockings, suspenders are much more satisfactory than garters.

They are more hygienic, inasmuch as they do not tend to restrict the circulation as in the case of a band of elastic drawn tightly round the leg.

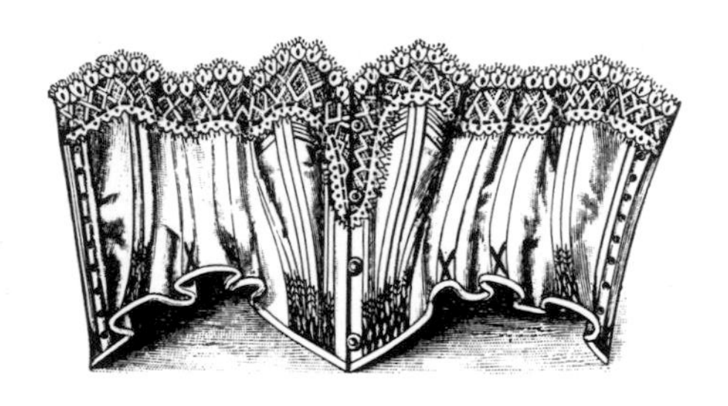

If suspenders are worn, it is always well to ensure that the studs are surrounded by some soft silk or kid covering, otherwise they are apt to tear the stockings, forming what is known as a 'ladder'.

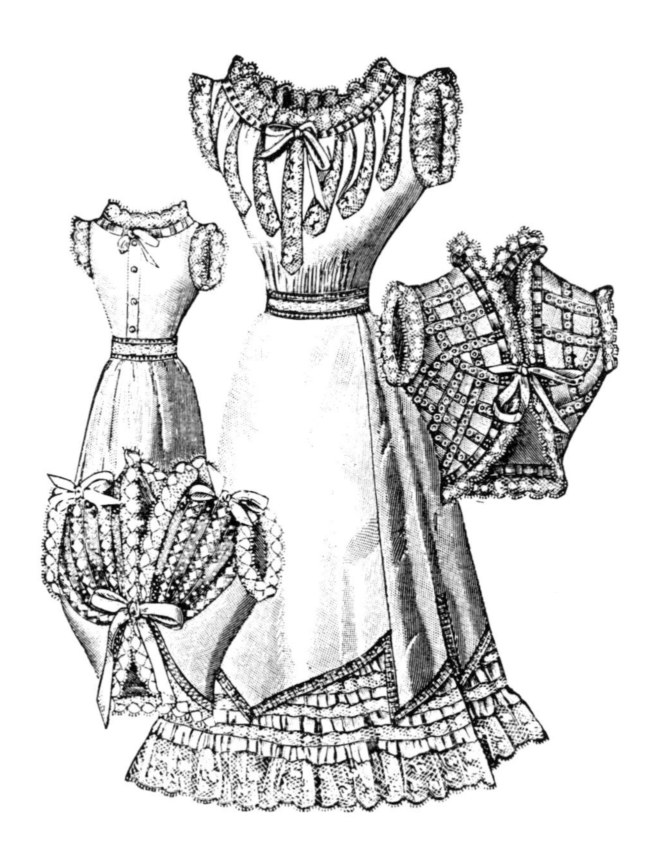

CONSIDERATIONS...

AGE
The fast fading attractions...

Good taste in dress is by no means above the consideration of older women. Of course there are some who *never* can imagine themselves old.

When a woman refuses to accept the fact that she is no longer young, it is not surprising that she should offend against good taste by dressing in a style utterly unsuited to her years.

So long as she looks neat and respectable, and displays a sufficient amount of expensive lace, diamonds, and so many yards of unexceptionable silk or satin, many people think that it little matters what a middle-aged lady wears.

As long as the face is fit to present itself to society, good taste should carefully attend the fast-fading attractions. Ringlets and roses, are appropriate to youth alone, but an arrangement of cap or head-dress is more becoming to the poor old ruins!

CONSIDERATIONS...

YOUTH

Needing little outward adornment...

There are rules for the young, which, if attended to, will prevent their offending against good taste. The freshness of youth has a beauty of its own which needs but little outward adornment.

The ravages of time have not to be repaired. Youth has charms of its own, and the more simply it is attired the better.

The young girl should never make herself conspicuous by her dress.

If she is beautiful, let her dress aid her beauty by not drawing away the attention from it.

If she is plain let her not attract all eyes to her plainness.

If attention is paid to these points there will be fewer of those startling peculiarities and eccentricities which offend against good taste.

RANK

Going without food for finery.

There is nothing more hateful than pretension. **Persons in humble class** of life will often ape their betters, dressing after them, and even going without necessary food in order to get some piece of finery!

Fine gowns of inconvenient length, silk mantles richly trimmed, often conceal the coarsest, scantiest, and most ragged underclothing.

Good taste may be exercised in the choice of suitable becoming colours and patterns. Good and useful things may also be pretty!

FOR THE SERVANTS

Finery will be no use...

Neatness and respectability of appearance are always required of servants; whether they have high or low wages, these qualities should be expected.

A servant's dress should be suited to her work. If she buy finery, it will be no use to her; she will only lay out a certain sum to look 'genteel'. This is a mistake, for finery is *not* gentility.

Servant-girls who can scarcely read, much less write, who do not know how to spell their names, who have low wages, and, as little children, had scarcely shoes to their feet; who, perhaps, never saw fresh meat in their homes except at Christmas, when it was given them by some rich neighbour - spend all their earnings on their dress!

Morning

Afternoon

£25 A YEAR

	£	s.	d.
One good costume	4	0	0
Summer dress	2	0	0
One afternoon dress	2	10	0
One evening dress	2	10	0
One wrap or coat	1	10	0
Boots and shoes	2	5	0
Hats	2	0	0
Blouses	2	0	0
Underclothing	3	10	0
Gloves, veils, neckwear	1	10	0
Umbrella or sunshade	0	10	0
Cleaning, boot-mending, &c.	0	15	0
	£25	0	0

£40 A YEAR

	£	s.	d.
One good costume	5	5	0
One best summer dress	3	0	0
Two lingerie dresses at £1 each	2	0	0
Afternoon dress	3	0	0
Evening dress	4	0	0
Wrap	2	10	0
Blouses	3	0	0
Underclothing (including dressing-gown)	5	0	0
Boots and shoes	3	0	0
Hats	3	0	0
Gloves, veils, and neckwear	2	10	0
Umbrella or sunshade	0	15	0
Repairing, cleaning, &c.	1	0	0
	£38	0	0

COST

Keeping up appearances.

The cost of dress depends so much on the prudence as well as on the discrimination of a lady.

The cost of a woman's wardrobe will of course depend upon the social circle in which she moves and the appearance which she has to keep up.

A lady's maid who is quick and efficient is the best friend a lady can have who wishes to dress well at a small expense. She saves her wages again and again!

Good wages can always be commanded by a steady lady's maid who is quick at her needle, and they who possess such a treasure will *never* be willing to part with her.

Those who earnestly desire to present a smart appearance must crush vanity - and minutely study not only their good points, but also their defects!
Having ascertained the latter, they must do all in their power to nullify and obliterate their existence.

HINTS FOR THE FIGURE - RULES:

If one shoulder is higher than the other, the coat or bodice must be cut to allow for this, and it should be so trimmed as to conceal this. A large collar, a fichu, or epaulettes all serve this purpose.

Those with high shoulders must eschew high sleeves, puffs, bows, and any sort of trimming at the top of the arm. Sleeves with the fullness drawn from the top half-way down to the elbow are desirable, and the drooping sleeve is most suitable of all.

Those possessing a thick, short neck must wear plain, tight, and neatly folded collars and bands, with, if desired, such trimming as the 'donkey's ear' fold, placed high up at the back of the neck; ruches or fussy collars of any sort are not suitable.

HINTS FOR THE FIGURE - RULES:

Women with long, angular, sharp elbows should never adopt a tight plain sleeve, as that style accentuates and calls attention to this defect. To such individuals there comes as 'a boon and a blessing', the ruched sleeve, sleeves formed of graduated tucks, sleeves with horizontal bands, and slashed sleeves.

Those desirous of concealing the length of their arms would do well to have their sleeves made of two materials - from the shoulder to the elbow, say, of velvet, and from elbow to wrist of silk.

The woman with long thin arms should under no circumstances adopt the plain tight sleeve with cuff falling over the hand - unless, of course, she desires to impress her acquaintances with her stick-like appendages!

HINTS FOR THE FIGURE - RULES:

The woman whose arms are too plump and short is almost more difficult to deal with than her slender sister, as it is far easier to increase than decrease proportions!

For the rounded shapely arm nothing is prettier than a plain sleeve brought up high on the shoulder with as pointed a cuff as possible falling over the hand. This effect is enhanced if the material is ribbed or striped, and if it is so arranged that the stripes meet in vertical points all along the outside edge of the sleeve.

Round-shouldered women must never indulge in perfectly plain 'backs'.

HOW TO AVOID DOWDINESS

Adopt a style that does not date quickly.

The well-dressed woman does not allow her appearance to become dowdy.

If her purse is limited she will adopt that style of dress that does not date quickly in preference to the most marked styles of the current season.

Simplicity should be the chief characteristic of the toilette of a woman of small means, and she should be careful to avoid bright colours.

Navy blue, black and other dark materials seldom 'date' a dress. The black costume may be varied with dressy blouses for dressy occasions, and simpler blouses for everyday wear, whilst varying little touches in the trimmings do wonders towards renovating a black dress.

A few more general hints in regard to colour may here be given.

THE CHOICE OF COLOUR

Many women are apt to nullify the effect of a really smart dress by selecting a colour which does not suit them.

It may be taken as a general rule that where the tints of the hair and eyes are repeated in the costume, the effect is on the whole successful. Thus, blue-eyed people rarely look so well as in the different shades of blue.

Fair girls with a delicate pink and white complexion looks well in the various soft subdued tones of pink.

Where the complexion is washed out anaemic or pale, white satin especially should be avoided.

The red or auburn haired woman must be particularly careful in her choice of colour. Green, for instance is considered an ideal colour, but it must be either a very dark green or a very faint delicate shade bordering on '*eau de nil*'. Brown and black may be worn, the low cut black evening gown serving to accentuate the whiteness of the skin.

THE CHOICE OF COLOUR

Dark haired women with sallow complexions look best in bright colours such as reds and yellows. Cream suits this style of complexion better than white.

Dark haired women with delicate fair skins require softer and less decided shades; white, dove greys, delicate pinks, or heliotrope are eminently suited to this style.

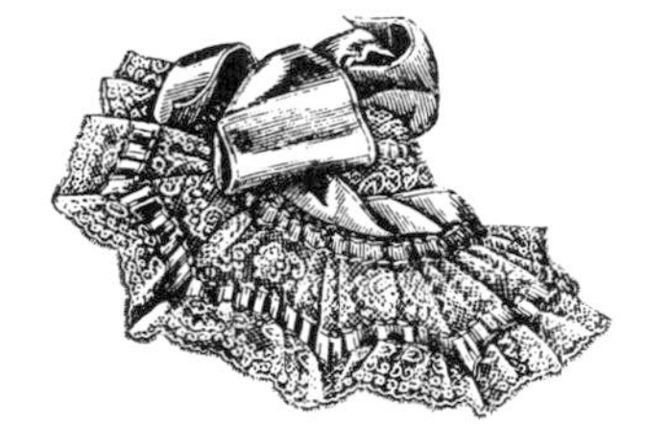

GOOD ADVICE

How to keep gloves clean when going out.

Light evening gloves are apt to become very quickly soiled. The wise woman will provide herself with a pair of cotton or woollen gloves (according to season) of a size larger than those she usually wears and slip them over her other gloves whilst travelling. She will of course, take them off when she reaches her destination, and the gloves underneath will be found to be quite clean and fresh, whereas if she had not taken this precaution they would have unavoidably become soiled.

New gloves.

Never put on a new pair of gloves hurriedly - work all the fingers into the glove fingers before putting in the thumb. It is as well to rest the elbow on the table while gently putting on the glove. A little powder dusted into the fingers of the gloves before putting them on will often make them go on more easily.

GOOD ADVICE

Creaking boots.

Well-made boots rarely creak; the creaking boot or shoe is usually one of an inferior quality. Standing the boots overnight in salt and water, using just sufficient cold water to cover the soles after rubbing a little oil well into the leather, will often remedy this annoying defect.

A word of warning to the middle aged woman

Very stiff and tight-fitting collars are injurious to the neck, causing it to become lined and often making the skin of an unbecoming yellow colour; these, like other extremes of fashion, should be avoided.

The Etiquette Collection is a series of pocket-sized books full of social secrets and hints for correct conduct. Collect the set!

THE ETIQUETTE OF NAMING THE BABY
Traditional names for your baby, their origins and meanings - and the people in history who have shared the names.

THE ETIQUETTE OF AN ENGLISH TEA
How to serve a perfect English afternoon tea; tea traditions, superstitions, recipes - including how to read your fortune in the tea-leaves afterwards.

THE ETIQUETTE OF ENGLISH PUDDINGS
Are you missing a good old-fashioned pudding? English puddings - the traditional way. Delicious recipes which have been used for over 100 years.

The Etiquette of Politeness
Good sense and good manners. How to be polite and well-bred at all times.

The Etiquette of Love & Courtship
A guide for romantics. Flirting, temptation, first impressions: essential advice for lovers.

Etiquette for Gentlemen
No real gentleman should be without these rules for correct conduct. A must for the gentleman in every woman's life!

Etiquette for Coffee Lovers
Coffee as it ought to be! Friends gathered over a steaming cup of coffee, or those indulging in a single cup will enjoy the story of coffee drinking, recipes and coffee chat.

For your free catalogue containing details of these and other Copper Beech Gift Books, write to:

Copper Beech Publishing Ltd
P O Box 159 East Grinstead Sussex England RH19 4FS

Copper Beech Gift Books
are designed and printed in
Great Britain.